6/00   9000854057

The Angelspeake Storybook

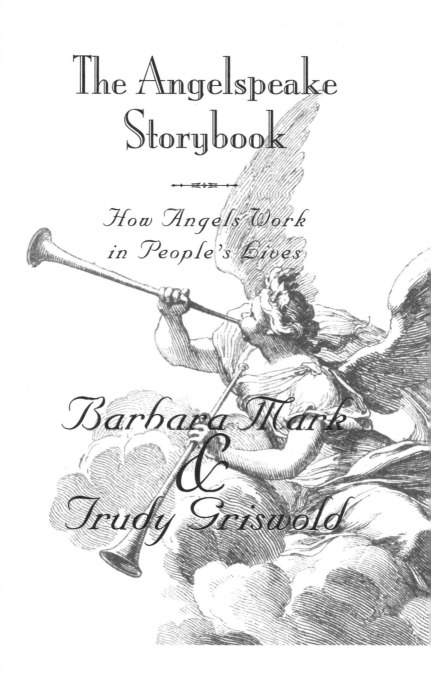

The Angelspeake Storybook

How Angels Work
in People's Lives

Barbara Mark
&
Trudy Griswold

Published by
Adams Media Corporation
260 Center Street, Holbrook, MA 02343

ISBN: 1-58062-250-X

Printed in the United States of America

J I H G F E D C B

Library of Congress Cataloging-in-Publication Data
Available from the publisher.

This book is available at quantity discounts for bulk purchases.
For information, call 1-800-872-5627.

Visit our home page at http://www.adamsmedia.com

Acknowledgments

———— ✠ ————

Terry DeFiore Wachtel—Who saw the possibilities and led the way.

James Nicholson—Who put the dream on paper and gave it shape.

Faith Craig and Cathy Subrisky—The most magnificent of support angels.

Amanda Borghese—Who shared her wisdom and experience so generously.

Jeff Herman—Who said "How about me?" when we asked.

Caroline Griswold, Suzanne Mark, and Linda Engstrom—Editors of the highest caliber.

Anne Weaver—Thanks for helping the angels find their way into the hearts of many.

Our dearest family—Who totally believe in us and in what we do.

And, above all, the deepest appreciation to all of you who made the extra effort to share your experiences with those who seek their angels.

We dedicate this book of stories to

Frances Shenker

&

Ralph Wachtel
for all you do . . .
we thank you

Contents

*Throughout your life you
have been blessed
with spiritual experiences,
brought by your angels.
Some are sacred and confidential.
Others, although sacred,
are meant to be shared.*

Introduction

—◄◆►—

Angels Do God's Work

—◄◆►—

When we sisters were in a business in the early '80s, we had a dear friend named Connie Hall. After being out of touch with her for many years, we found out that she had moved away from Atlanta and gotten married. We missed her, but since we didn't know her married name, we had no idea where to start looking for her. One night we were reminiscing about our friendship and since we ask the angels for help in nearly everything we do, we facetiously said, "Angels, have Connie Hall call us!"

One week to the day after our request for help to find Connie, there was a message on the answering machine that said, "Hi, this is Connie Hall Knight. I have been thinking about you two all week and thought I would try your number. I am living in Singapore."

Why were we surprised? The angels have helped us in every way imaginable and renewing an old friendship was no problem for them at all. That incident started us thinking about the many ways the angels aid us in our lives. We, who teach people to ask the angels for help at any time, still find ourselves amazed at the many ways the angels help us and work for us.

We also started thinking about what exactly the angels do, and we made a list of the daily ways they assist us. In small, large, silly, or serious ways, they are there. Sometimes we see clearly how they work, but most of the time, we don't understand the obvious ways we are supported. We forget that the angels are always there, always available, always willing, and always working for us.

From our own experiences in working with the angels, we made a list of how the angels operated in our own lives and entitled it "What Angels Do." People seemed to be curious about how angels worked, and we wanted to clarify angelic methods of helping so our readers and students could feel more aware of their own angelic experiences. We liked our list so much, that we decided to make each item a chapter title for *The Angelspeake Storybook*.

What Angels DO

Angels Do God's Work
Angels Love
Angels Teach
Angels Comfort
Angels Support
Angels Protect

Angels do a lot of things, but they will not take away your free will or the lessons you are here on earth to learn. If you make mistakes, in any aspect of living, the angels support you. Angels are also aware that life is not black or white, and if they were to give pat answers in their guidance, they would be taking away your freedom of choice. Angels rarely give yes or no answers. They don't judge, scold, preach, or give advice you don't ask for. Angelic messages are always loving!

As God's messengers, the angels bring us truth, peace, and love while doing their work. How they do that is what creates the stories that people tell us. That is what this book is about.

We were taught to call God a "He," but whatever you call God—a He, She, or It—the angels sent by God come here to do the work He wants done. We are calling God a "He" in this book, because that is the standard in our culture.

Spiritual events on this earth seem to be happening on an even grander scale than before. Either that or we are more aware of how God and His angels work in our lives more than at any time in the past. Frankly, we aren't sure which it is — maybe both. But one thing we do know, people are sharing their stories more openly. There is still a great propensity for people to tack on qualifying phrases to the stories. "This is weird," or "I have never told anyone else about this," or "You'll think I'm crazy, but . . ."

The best part about writing our books is the connection we make with other spiritually aware people. We feel as though we have spiritual "angel buddies" all over the world. And we do. Like-minded people are everywhere. People needing to share their love of the angels come to us in every way. We receive phone calls, e-mail, snail mail, and faxes every day which include short stories about how angels have changed lives or simply given someone a laugh or a new perspective. Many students share their personal angel messages with us and relate to us the results of that communication.

We believe all the stories we receive. We know angels work in strange and mysterious ways. We were both sound asleep when the angels woke us up. Both of us, at different times, in different parts of the United States, were living our lives, with no background or awareness of any particular spiritual gift about to arrive. All of a sudden we were catapulted into an awareness that totally changed us, our families, and our idea of ourselves. It was never the same after the day we were awakened. Our story was "weird" to us at first, too.

People who acknowledge their angels' help aren't crazy. If we were, we would certainly be in good company. This book will help you understand that people all over the world are having angel experiences just like you are. In fact, angel contact seems to be a unifying force. We have noticed that no matter where an angel message is received or the culture or religion of the one who receives it, the messages are similar. Angels love, teach, comfort, encourage, support, and help you feel safe.

The Angelspeake Storybook is another means of learning how angels touch your lives and what angels do to help you. Angels support all beliefs. So, if some of the stories are not what you believe, or agree with, just know that your angels will support your unique beliefs, too. No matter where you are in your spiritual process, you will be able to relate to the fun, joy, wisdom, and truth this book shares. This little storybook comes at the request of hundreds of readers who have asked to learn more about how angels work and what they do.

All of us have a need to share how the angels have touched us, spoken to us, taught us, or inspired us. We want to talk about it! Perhaps you have been thinking that you were the only one who has had an angelic experience. You are not alone.

Angels come to everyone. They come to you, too. Many of the people who write to us have already been communicating with their angels—or angelspeaking—usually because they have read our books, *Angelspeake: How to Talk with Your Angels*, and *The Angelspeake Book of Prayer and Healing*. Others have seen us on TV, or have participated in a workshop or seminar. But about a third of the people who contact us have been talking with their angels for some time on their own and are very excited to find like-minded angel friends.

Many times, when friends would say, "I have an angel story for you," we would answer, "Write it down! Just like you told it to us. Write it down!" Many of you did! Others were reluctant to do so because they were afraid that the spelling wouldn't be right or the grammar would be off. We don't care about that. We love the stories. The angels encourage all of us to share how they help us, for it is in the sharing that angels become more and more real in our lives.

Angels are helpful. When we learn how to work with them, they can be even more helpful. They have already taught us the Four Fundamentals for accessing angels to help us with anything we wanted to be, to do, or to have in our lives. For you who want to speak to your angels, here is the simple method our angels taught us. It is easy to learn to receive your own written communication from your personal angelic support team.

Speaking with your angels is easier than you may think. Your angels want to connect with you even more than you want to connect with them. Here are four simple steps that thousands of people just like you have followed to live a fulfilled spiritual life.

Four Fundamentals

1. **Ask:** Say a prayer and invite your angels to be with you and to wrap you in the loving light of God. Sit quietly with paper and pencil in hand. Be open and allow the exchange of energy to come through to you.

2. **Believe and Trust:** Your angels are with you and you will receive a message. Let it happen. You are being guided although you may feel you are making it up. The message will seem like your own thoughts. Acceptance is most important.

3. **Let Go:** Begin writing what you know to write. Let the angelic energy come through to you. It may be as a soft whisper, a picture in your mind, or a feeling of knowing. Your angels have the same loving voice you have heard many times before. The harder you think, the less flow there will be.

4. **Say Thank You:** You have received a spiritual gift for which you didn't have to do anything. Simply be grateful for what you have received and acknowledge receiving it by giving thanks.

A Beginning Prayer

Angels sent by God to guide me, be my light
and walk beside me.
Be my guardian and protect me. On the paths
of life direct me. Amen

--- ⋯≡◈≡⋯ ---

Everybody feels as though they are making their
angel message up at first. We wish we had a nickel
for every phone call we received saying, "I think I
am making it up." It is natural because writing to
your angels is different and new. But when you
write in spite of the feeling of making it up, you
will get a message. The message is in your heart,
not your head. So write what you know to write
and believe it is the angels.

As Trudy told Barbara when we first began to
write and felt like *we* were making it up, "Well,
who cares? It's good stuff. Let's just keep it coming!" It has never stopped.

Most of the "divine intervention" stories you
read about in books and that are related on television are pretty dramatic. And yet, it is the intimacy
of the small stories or the little moments when you
knew your angels were there and helping you that

really make believers out of the most doubting skeptics. Angels are not only with you to save your life when you are in danger, they are *in* your life every single moment in every way imaginable.

To help keep things clear in this storybook, our writings and our contributors' stories are in regular print. The angels' messages, quotes, and teachings are in red italics.

We are creating a forum through *The Angelspeake Storybook* to relate your story. When you tell someone your story, it becomes more real; the understanding of how the angels' work increases and the world becomes a better place. There are many others being awakened by their angels. The next time you are sitting next to a total stranger, ask, "Do you believe in angels?" You may be amazed at what you hear.

This morning, as we worked on this Introduction, the angels woke us up early to give us a start with this message.

"Angels, why did you wake us up?" we asked.

They answered with excitement in their energy, *Because today is a very important day. We are here in droves to work with you to write/finish this new testimonial of our love for humankind and to teach that we help people. That is your message in this book.* **We help people!** *Your mission is to record the myriad ways in which we can help, be accessed and trusted. Yes, trusted! For many times we help, but our help is denied. Teach in this book to accept what is given. Accept God by accepting our help. Speed up your progress by asking for us to help you.*

Evidently the angels did not want us to miss the point that they help people, because our friend, Amanda, called us shortly after to read this message to us. We end our Introduction, as we do all chapters, with a special angel quotation.

We are here to help you help others. That's what you want and what we want. You don't need more when you give gifts of LOVE to others. ASK, ASK, ASK us to help you and you will not believe what you will accomplish.

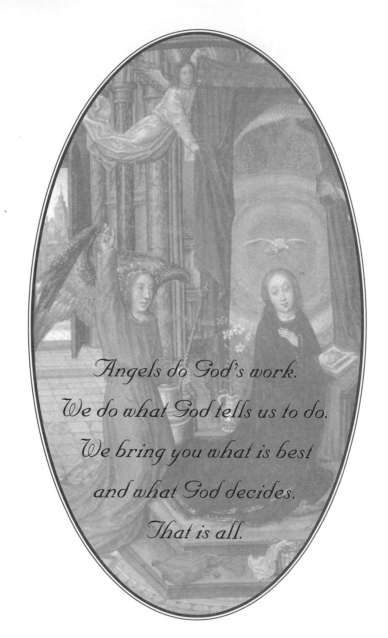

Angels do God's work.

We do what God tells us to do.

We bring you what is best

and what God decides.

That is all.

Chapter 1

Angels are God's Messengers

Angels do God's work. If you want to look at it from a human perspective, God assigns helpers to carry out His plans. So He has designed angels to be on earth (and every other planet in the universe), to carry out His infinite number of directives.

God sends His angelic messengers to do the things He requires. Angels are documented back to 5000 B.C. If you go to the Louvre or any other archeological museum, especially in the Middle East, you will see statues and artifacts depicting angels. At the foot of Pharaoh, there are angels pictured. Hammurabi, the lawgiver and founder of the first Babylonian dynasty, is shown in sculpture with a very small angel on his shoulder while delivering part of his famous code. The physical presence and acknowledgment of angels in writing and art, is well documented throughout the ages. Angels appeared to Noah. Jacob wrestled with an angel, was transformed, and his name was changed to Israel. God sent angels to Mary, the mother of Jesus. He sent angels to announce His plans in every culture and religion, and He sends His angels to help people like you and me, too.

FIRST E-MAIL FROM TANKSAMILLION

I was looking for a book for my wife at the Singapore Airport and I chose *The Angelspeake Book of Prayer and Healing.* She is a devout Christian and the most honest person I know. I am not a Christian, although I have always believed in God's existence. I had read but part way through the second chapter when I was moved to realize that I could actually pray. The barriers were no longer there. I wanted to connect with God!

I then felt compelled to call my wife at once from the airport just to let her know how I was feeling. I don't know if she felt it, but there were a few tears welling in my eyes.

As I kept reading your book, I wanted to thank you and the angels who are looking after me. I know I have asked before and I know I have very often received, but you've shown me how it has happened. I do not know as yet where this will lead me, but I am sure I will find my way into His great plan for me.

I thank you and thank you and thank you. Perhaps that is why I chose my Internet username of "tanksamillion."

Second E-mail from Tanksamillion

(One month later.)
Thank you for your e-mail reply. You were right, I have been awakened and my old beliefs have been left behind. Today I received my baptism. This was much to the surprise of my wife when I told her of my intention a few days ago. She and a group of her friends had prayed, without my knowledge, for eight long years for this day!

Deborah's Story

At first I was skeptical that I could talk to my angels. I was one of those who thought they were making it up. Now I am amazed at the responses I've gotten.

Zacarias, Raphael, and Sunshine have become my constant angelic companions. I talk to them all the time. It's like having a running conversation going on in the back of my mind. They give me so many wonderful insights it's hard to count them all. The two best gifts they've given me are the ability to accept who I am without judgement attached and I have met my very dear new friend.

My new friend had to have been sent by the angels. Our backgrounds are extremely different, but our viewpoints and tastes are remarkably similar. The first time I met her I surprised myself when I blurted out, "I talk to angels." She said, "Tell me more." Now she "angelspeakes" and I discovered that watching the reaction of someone who has just made the "connection" is just as joyful as "connecting" myself. Sharing our writings with each other has added a depth to our experience.

I now look forward to each day to see what new wonders it will bring—and it always does.

KAREN'S E-MAIL

Several months ago, I read that angels want to let us know they are with us. The book I was reading suggested that you ask your angel for something— a sign, if you will.

I read this on a Wednesday night. On Thursday morning I said to my angel, "OK, if you are really there, I would like some flowers." Now, my husband has given me fresh flowers only three times in twenty years. It was the middle of winter, and there was certainly nothing in the garden. I didn't tell anyone in my family about this.

All day Thursday, I thought about my angel and the flowers. By afternoon, I was beginning to think I had been a bit unreasonable. After all, how are angels supposed to acquire flowers? Maybe I had asked for something too difficult. So, I spoke to my angel again. "I think I gave you a difficult assignment. If I get a card in the mail with a flower on it, or even a catalog from a mail-order nursery, I'll count it."

Thursday night I went to sleep, admittedly a little let down, as there were no flowers in sight. At 6:30 the next morning my exercise partner came to my door as usual. In her arms was a bouquet of pink carnations for me!

I am a believer.

We have always been a spiritual family. When we took nature walks together, I would explain to my four-year-old son that the sounds, such as the wind in the trees, were God's way of talking to us and that we must hush to hear. Statements such as this were commonplace in our family.

One evening as I tucked my son into bed, he announced intensely, but peacefully, "I took a walk with God today, Mommy."

I offhandedly answered, "That's nice, honey. Did you have a nice walk?"

He continued, "We went to a place where there were colors that were better than my crayons. It was so beautiful!"

At this point I started listening more intently and said, "What did God look like?" By this time I thought my child might have had a legitimate spiritual experience.

"Well, He came to me like He was seven years old so I wouldn't be scared by how big He was. I knew it was God, though, and that I didn't need to be scared. He showed me the beautiful place and He said how much you and Daddy love me and that He loves me, too."

He kept on talking about his wonderful walk with God, but his last comment convinced me his experience was real. "Oh, Mommy, I saw a light there that was the brightest light I have ever seen. I could look right into it but it didn't hurt my eyes."

I asked him what the light was, and He casually answered, like everyone should know it, "The light was love."

Keep in mind this was a young child who, at that time, had no experience with such things. He had no reference point to make these statements. I have no doubt in my mind that my son did, indeed, walk with God that day.

E-MAIL FROM MCL

This morning I was driving to work anticipating a humdinger of a day. As I drove I said out loud, "God, send me an angel to help me to get through all I have to do today."

When I arrived at my office I turned on the lights and spotted the most adorable little angel doll hanging from a suction cup and sticking to my computer screen. A clerk in the office had purchased it for me.

That was not the first time that while driving to work, I have asked God to send me an angel, only to arrive there and find an angel token waiting for me. So if anyone ever doubts if God hears you, YES! He certainly does. Our angelic friends will let us know they are there in some pretty special ways.

JOAN'S STORY

One night I was suddenly awakened from a sound sleep to find these shooting balls of light flying all over the room. They were *not* reflections from outside. There were balls of light flying around. I got scared and dove under the covers. When I got up enough nerve to peek out from under the blankets, they were still there—flying all over the place. This went on for about an hour. Me peeking out—them flying around. They were little white shooting balls of light. That is the only way I can explain them. They didn't stop until I paid attention to them and "listened" to what they wanted me to know. And that was to study about God and the angels. That incident was the beginning of a whole new way of thought in my life and the start of my spiritual studies. My whole life has been different since.

R. Williams Writes

I am a Christian woman and being more acutely aware of God's angels being present in my life has given me great comfort. Actually, it's very exciting. It has made me realize that God is much more powerful and awesome than our human minds realize. I feel that I have received three very short, succinct messages from my angel or angels. I knew that these messages were from God because, for example, one of the messages just came into my mind when I wasn't even inquiring about a particular subject.

I was sitting down to lunch one Sunday after church, and the message *"You eat too much because you are angry,"* came into my mind. I had prayed and inquired about that issue a few days earlier. Even though the message was blunt, it was very comforting to me to receive it, because I have been searching for the answer to why I have gained weight.

The Lord has impressed upon me to do as much as I can in my life, out of love. I also feel more secure about having God's guidance come to me whenever I pray or God feels it is appropriate.

From Carolyn

So many great things have happened in my life because of the angels. I have finally listened to God telling me that He wants me to share my knowledge with others. So, I have begun giving classes at my home in positive self-centering that God gave the name "The Path." We work on mind, body, and spirit. The idea is to learn how to walk on the path that God presents for us in our life for greater happiness and to stay centered within ourselves.

I cannot tell you how wonderful my life has been since I truly learned how to walk in God's light and follow His directions.

From Michelle

I first saw you and your sister on TV but couldn't watch because I was busy being a mom. That night, after thinking more about the show, all I could remember was you saying pray and write what you know, and to ask a question. I said a prayer, took some deep breaths, and began to write. When I stopped, I couldn't remember what I had written! I felt a feeling like chills. Peace, calm, strength, and more all rolled into one feeling.

I have written to my angels every night since. I am calmer and more patient with my son. I have a better feeling of self. I am looking at the world through clearer eyes. I look back on my life when I have prayed for things and gotten them. I said thank you, but just went on with life. The angels' writing help me realize that my angels are with me no matter what. I love this feeling!

——⋅⋅——

No one is too big or too insignificant to be over-looked by God and His angels. Believe this. When God's helpers come to us, they are giving love to us, teaching us, healing us, supporting us, protect-ing us, and communicating with us. All at the same time. The way in which they appear or make themselves known is very special and personal. Be aware of your divine helpers and how they come to you.

We angels are loving helpers that band together in all types of situations to aid and assist when assistance is needed. You can depend on us to be there for you when you need us.

Love yourself unconditionally. True, pure love is a growing thing that evolves as you evolve.

Chapter 2

Angels Love

There is a phrase we often hear when people begin to receive messages from their angels. "I have never felt so much love," is how they explain their experience. There seems to be an acute awareness and a quickening of our cells when an angel's love energy flows through us. When people begin to feel their angel's energy around them, they frequently feel like they want to cry because the feeling of love is so overwhelming.

Angels teach us to love and to love well. The sayings "On earth as it is in heaven," or "As above, so below," relate to love. For as God loves us, the angels will teach us to love God, each other, and ourselves.

Angels frequently show us their love by some sort of sign, sometimes a touch. It is impossible to miss it when an angel touches you. People may feel shivers, goosebumps, joy, or peace and calm. Your experience will be uniquely yours. The angels have told us to use the phrase "love-rush" to explain how it feels when an angel is affirming your experience or sending healing. Everything is perfect. This verse from the angel's poem, "Angeltouches," really describes a "love-rush" well.

Angeltouches

Think of a time when an idea came to you
that was so pure and was so true for you
rolls of shivers started in one part
of your body and
then inundated every cell of your being.
You may call that
Angeltouches
Or
Loverushes.
That was Us.

A LETTER FROM J. ST. JOHN

I'm sitting alone, my baby is sleeping, I have just watched your video and I had to write. At your ending prayer the hairs on my whole body felt like someone tickling me. I even laughed because it felt so tingly.

When I began to write, *Dearest Child, we love you and. . .* I just broke down and cried and cried and I couldn't write. I felt engulfed in this tingly, goosebump feeling and I could hear, *"It's okay, it's okay,"* over and over and over. Then I heard, *"Everything will be all right."* I turned off the video and prayed to God and cried some more. I have never had so many tears fall from my eyes.

I then welcomed the angels into my home, my life, and my children's lives. I also asked for a sign to show me they were with me and not that it was just stress that was making me cry so hard.

Then I turned the video on again and you asked the group, "Did anyone feel like crying?" I started crying again! Then I visualized for a quick second (that seemed like a lifetime) what it would look like inside a pair of beautiful white angel wings. I felt like an angel was behind me and he was wrapping his wings totally around me in an enormous hug. Am I crazy?

I have books and books on angels, but I have never read about an experience like this. I had to tell you right away. I can't wait to finish the video, but I have to stop crying first. It seems like I am crying for everything I have had bottled up inside me for a long, long time. It is such a relief.

Thank you and God bless you!

Angels don't always show their love in a physical way. Sometimes they show how special they think you are by deeds or actions. Hearing an unexpected favorite song on the radio may really be a type of "angel hug." Watch for synchronistic events that bring a chuckle or a little joy to you through a little angelic intervention. This is how they show us they love us and want to be sure we don't miss it.

LETTER FROM EILEEN

My angels love me! I know this in my heart. They even have a pet name for me—they call me Little One. They have been so patient with me because I've had a hard time just letting them handle things when I've invoked their help. One night I was feeling especially low and alone, feeling that they didn't hear me and didn't care. I picked up *The Angelspeake Book of Prayer and Healing*, and opened right to pages 66–67. What I read made me cry tears of relief. It was about learning to let it happen and developing patience. What lifted the sadness was the part I read over and over—*"It is not necessary to keep asking, praying, or begging. Allow. Allow. Allow. Be still and know that God has received your request and is working on it. You have not been forgotten."*

I thought I had truly understood the message of *Angelspeake*, but it wasn't until that moment that I *knew* what I should do. The request I made of them hasn't been granted yet, but I will let you know when it is. Notice I said "when" and not "if"! This is what my angels have taught me so far—just believe and let it happen. They've also told me I've done very well so far and that we have many bridges to cross together.

I can hardly wait to see what my angels will show me next. I'm excited about the future because I truly understand now that I'm not alone, and that everything wonderful and joyful can be mine thanks to my beloved angels. I love them so much that my heart is overflowing.

A CHAT ABOUT LOVE BETWEEN PAEGE AND HER ANGELS

Paege: I have a question, angels. I am lonely and wish I had a mate.

Angels: *Of course you do. You are a loving person and wish for someone to share that with. It is God's way.*

Now, why do you not think you are lovable enough to attract a desirable mate? Because at times you have been unloving, and therefore felt unlovable. You are learning to erase the one and enhance the other. It is not easy to do this. It is a careful balance between inner and outer, between good and bad. Between giving and receiving. Between male and female. Both parts of both people.

Paege: I do feel unlovable a lot of the time.

Angels: *It is very hard on earth to know love truly. Many, many times there have been no concepts in your society for what love truly is. Today you have a much more spiritual concept than ever before. Therefore you cannot find love because you are seeking in the old ways for a new thought and concept only recently taught to you.*

Paege: How will I recognize a true love then?

Angels: *Here is the truth for spiritual beings who seek love.*

Only God can bring your love to you. You have tried to pick a love in the past and look what it has gotten you. You can only receive from God the gift of true, pure love. Humans are not able to recognize it. For true, pure love is a growing thing that evolves as the soul evolves. You will only know it when you give up all hope of finding it. For the very act of wanting it keeps it away.

Paege: I haven't picked my love relationships very well in the past, which is what scares me.

Angels: *Know this, Child. God is aware of your plea. And know this also—there is another—the other half of you—that is also yearning for a true love. You are being drawn together, not by the seeking of each other, but by the gift and love of God. It is a beautiful occurrence that is happening even today. Do not worry about seeking or finding. Only live today in the most loving and generous of manners, and all will be brought to you easily, totally and generously.*

Paege: I don't want to miss anything.

Angels: *Rejoice in the Love of God for now. For that love will direct you to other loves and the circle will complete and you will KNOW when it does. You are as married today to your lifemate as if you shared your heart and had taken your vows. There is not apartness within you. You already know each other and are preparing to meet. It is very good.*

Suz and Ed's story

Ed's version:

I must begin this amazing story of love by reflecting on the days of my childhood. It was a time when I felt close to God. It was a time when inspirational thoughts—angel thoughts—were a common occurrence. These private thoughts made me strong and fearless.

Then came adolescence and other realities entered into my life as I moved into adulthood. I was bombarded with adult magazines and movies that emphasized the sensual aspects of life. This is when I made the decision to quit listening to the angel thoughts, which seemed childish compared to the sophisticated, sensual stuff I was learning. I went through high school, military service, college, and graduate school, still with the idea that life was really about self-satisfaction.

I had enjoyed country & western dancing for some time and usually frequented a certain dance place. But on one Tuesday night, it occurred to me not to go there, but to go to another place. Was this an angel thought? I turned off my usual course and went to the other place.

It was there that I met an interesting group of people. They stood out of the crowd because none of them was smoking or drinking. One woman in particular caught my eye, but every time I tried to get her to dance, someone beat me to it. Finally I got my chance. Her name was Suz.

I asked her to dance. She accepted, and as the music started and we touched, something powerful, and do I dare say magical, was happening. The music that before was loud, now, with us linked hand-in-hand seemed to soften and the pace seemed slower. It was at this moment that I knew beyond all doubt Suz was the love of my life—my forever partner. Along with this instant knowing, I heard the word "patience."

It seemed none of these things was apparent to Suz. When I asked her about a date sometime, she simply said, "No, I'm not dating right now." Several other times I asked her out and was turned down. Nor would she give me her phone number.

Then the first week in January I saw her again and she indicated that we needed to get off the dance floor to talk. We found a table as far from the music as possible and sat down. She proceeded to explain that before she could even talk about dating anyone, certain issues had to be discussed. As I remember, these issues were God, chastity, religion, drinking, and so forth. I realized these issues were important to me, too.

At the time I was drinking a beer, and after her introductory statement, I got up and threw it away. (By the way, that was the last drink of alcohol I ever had!) I went back to the table, sat down, looked her in the eyes, and said, "Try me!" I was so moved by the freedom of her action, that I wanted to know what she knew.

Our discussion continued throughout the evening, covering many spiritual aspects of life. By the end of the evening, she gave me her phone number on a napkin. I was thrilled.

As my relationship with God and the angels quickly unfolded, so did Suz's and mine. By the end of February I asked her to be my bride. The angels intervened here again. We were each reassured in

many ways and levels that this was a match made in heaven. On March 9, 1990, we were united for what we are sure is a holy purpose. We listen together for heavenly inspiration to guide our every moment. We trust we are about "our Father's business."

Suz's version:

In 1989, three years after having gone through a drawn-out divorce and having been left a single parent of three children, I started to receive spontaneous angel messages which could only be characterized as amazingly hopeful, joyous, comforting, and practical.

One evening while on an outdoor walk, I was struck head to toe with a beautiful sense of light and happiness. Almost simultaneously I "heard" this message: *It is done!* Suddenly the word "done" was defined for me in biblical proportions. I was convinced that God had done something amazing on my behalf, and that I needed to be patient and to listen for further guidance.

And more came. Not long after, I saw a woman with a beautiful wedding ring on. The angel message clicked into my mind, *"You are just as married as she is."* Again the message came with a sense of joy and peace.

My relationship with God was growing so real and precious to me. I realized that it was a kind of ideal relationship in which I felt loved, no matter what I looked like, felt like, or sounded like. God was always there for me. I was beginning to understand that my ideal marriage should be like my relationship with God and that somehow such a relationship was ALREADY mine because I understood this. I was filled with joy even though it was not related to an actual man in my life, for there was no future husband anywhere within sight, as far as I could tell.

I guess I had little venetian blinds pulled over my eyes. In January, several of my group went country & western dancing. A man in a gray cowboy hat, who had asked me out several times, asked me out again. But before I said no, yet another time, an angel message stopped me short. *"Why not be honest and kind and tell him* why *you have always said no."*

To my amazement, the following words poured out of my mouth, "To even consider one date with someone, I want that someone to really understand me. And to do this we would have to have long talks about issues that mean a lot to me—like pre-marital chastity, drinking, God, etc." This man calmly got up from the table and walked away with his beer. I thought, "Well, I guess that is one way to screen out those who are not really interested in who I am."

Moments later he reappeared with water, not beer. He sat down and said, "Try me!" The rest of the evening we talked about everything we could think of. We were among the last to leave and I felt, as we exchanged phone numbers, that I had just met my best friend!

In the next month or two my angel messages assured me that his motives were True, Good, and Enduring—words God had told me were the greatest description of what a marriage and a husband should have. And that here was the relationship that matched the one I had with Him.

We were married in March. We know we have been put together for some divine purpose. Daily we listen for angel messages, and eagerly share what we have heard.

SUZANNE M'S STORY

I attended Barbara and Trudy's angel seminar in Vermont and the whole weekend was truly amazing. The last day of the seminar, they wanted us to draw our angel. They gave us crayons and paper and this cynical little voice inside me said, "Yeah, right, you want me to do what? This will not work. No way!" But, since I actually like to draw, I decided to give it a try.

Well, I got the crayons and paper and started to draw an angel. It didn't look like any angel I thought I would have. It was a bald, muscular man with beautiful violet and green eyes. I thought, "Hmmm, I wonder how I made this up?" At the same moment as my thought, I looked into those eyes. All of a sudden, WHAM! I felt this incredible rush of the purest, most powerful love I had ever experienced and I started to cry.

I can only describe the feeling I was experiencing as I looked at my picture as one of shame. I felt unworthy to receive such deep unconditional love. All of my feelings of unworthiness and pain were being burned out by the glory of God's love through this angel drawing. It was an incredibly healing love and my life has not been the same since. Now, every day I feel more whole and more worthy of God's love and I now know that is what the angels are for—to teach us how precious and loved we are and to heal our deepest loneliness and pain. I am so grateful.

Love is the closest a human can get to knowing how an angel feels inside. Love is the greatest thing there is. That is what angels are here to give you. They help us with many things, but at the root of everything they offer and help us with is love.

Love is everything we do. There is no angel contact of any kind without love, for that is what we are. We have no fear within us. We have no ego. We have no sadness or judgement. We are love. Angels love. It is not easy to imagine the love that angels have for you. It is hard to fully imagine a being whose whole existence is to connect you with God. It is hard to understand such devotion and constancy. Love is what we are.

Today,
ask your angel for help.
Let us take some of the
pressure off you.
Let us teach you.

Chapter 3

Angels Teach

Angels give perspective. No matter how difficult, hopeless, or joyless your life seems, the angels will teach you how to return to strength and happiness. Angels help us understand why we are here on earth and to remember what our purpose is. They know our life purpose and remember what we want to accomplish. We humans can only see the smaller picture.

Angels see how people interrelate and how one event leads to another. You may only know about your family tree two or three generations back, but the angels can trace your lineage back to the beginning and see the rhythms, the ebbs, the flows, and the reasons you are together now.

When you get lost and don't know where you are or what to do next, trust your angels to help get you back on track through their teachings. We like this simple request, "Dear Angels, help me know where to put my foot down next. Please make it REALLY clear, so I won't miss it." There is learning at both ends of life's spectrum and on every level. The angels are around to maximize all learning possibilities.

When your life is good or on an uphill swing, the angels will be there to share in your laughter and to maximize your success, too. They will teach you how to enjoy the good times, just as they help you with the difficult times.

FROM MARY T.

My life has sure gotten better since I started writing my angels!

I asked for a teaching angel the other day because I was looking for some serious instruction. My angel, who calls me "Luv" and "Child," said he was not a teacher but an instructor because teaching indicated there was something only he knew whereas an instructor imparted information given to him especially for me. He was quite eloquent. So, from now on, I guess I will ask for my instructing angel.

An Angel Message for Stephen

Stay in the now. Stay in today. Today is a good day with many wonderful and beautiful things in it. If you wish to feel better, breathe, breathe, breathe. Cleanse yourself with breath. You are feeling poorly in your stomach because you are not releasing your anxieties. That is what breath does. Breathing is the same as flooding dirt away with gallons and gallons of water. Same with breath. You will clear away a great deal of stress with cleansing breaths. Stop, now, and breathe.

Fax from Charlotte

Here is what the angels taught me when I was writing to them this morning.

Dear Angels, Can you explain the message again that you gave me about the way you work with us when we ask you a question?

Yes, it is really quite simple. Your mind is, of course,

made up of the conscious, sub-conscious, and the super-conscious. The super-conscious is your God-self and knows all things already. When you communicate with us, we send through your super-conscious the answers you need to hear. When you trust and believe in the messages, your sub-conscious goes to work and you can't fail. The key is Trust and Belief. YOU *make it happen!*

Always and forever,
Your angels

AN E-MAIL FROM RAE ELLEN

I am not done with your book yet. I went through about one-half of it last night and was so over-whelmed with the answers it was directing at me, for me. I went to bed and awoke at 4:30 in the morning. By 5:30 I had started writing my angels. They were so excited to be in touch with me. I couldn't write fast enough. There were some parts I didn't want to write because it was such good stuff about me and sounded egotistical. They told me to, *"Write it!"*

The entire experience was, well, great! I have been told before that I have healing talents, gifts, tendencies, whatever. The angels fully confirmed this and will be instructing me to develop my gifts.

CINDY'S STORY

I am an author and I had finished my latest novel and passed it to my teacher and mentor for critique. She liked everything about it but the ending, which she said was awful. She told me she didn't know what I could do about it, but it was boring and I would never sell the novel to a publisher as it stood. I didn't have a clue as to how to fix the problem, as I was quite satisfied with the ending I had written and didn't see any other way the story could possibly conclude. I decided to sit down and meditate on the problem.

I had learned from Barbara's class that not only could we appeal to our angels for help but also individuals who had passed on. One of my favorite writers had been the late John D. MacDonald. Not really expecting anything, I asked my angels to ask John D. MacDonald how he would have ended my book.

I was amazed when images immediately flashed in my mind of an alternative ending, much more exciting, dramatic, and satisfying than my first one. It was like watching a movie. Not only was I shown the new ending, but I was shown how I had already set up the new happenings previously in the novel. I dashed to my computer, wrote the new ending, and rushed the whole package off to my editor. She called the day she had received the manuscript with an offer to buy it!

LENNAE'S SHARING

Your goal to encourage angel awareness is so important. Lots of angels are out there right now, urgently seeking us. This isn't news to you or probably anyone who reads angel periodicals, but I fell upon it just two years ago when I encountered my own guardian angel. She told me that millions of angels were surrounding the earth.

One evening, I felt strongly drawn to sit on my bed and write. Soon I became gripped with the warmest, most loving feeling I have ever felt. A tall column of light appeared, glowing brightly down through the ceiling. I couldn't see my dresser through its shimmering cloud. Pure energy seemed to fill every cell in my body yet I felt entirely safe and loved. Then I heard an unmistakably feminine voice: *"I am your guardian angel."*

I asked if she'd been making herself known to me this past week. I was clearly told yes and that her name was Paula. At that point, I started shaking with reverence and made my way into a room with a big mirror, to see if I was still here! My angel followed and I asked why I was being honored with her presence. She revealed, *"Over one million angels of peace are surrounding the earth and if humans listen to them, the earth will be saved. You will be able to let this and more be known."*

In a joyful but tearful voice I asked, "Why me? Why not choose my Mother—she's a saint." Her answer was, *"Don't be afraid. You are not alone. Many are being called to personally assist in spreading this love. And you are a wonderful person."*

Three days later, Paula prompted me to write down another message. *"Give your love—generously. Create beauty. Manage your energy!"* If we would all just start each day with these three 'simple' rules.

My intuitions have been especially keen since the ecstatic encounter with my angel. Many helpful and unexplained things have happened, such as being led to an unlocked gate around an apartment swimming pool where little ones would surely have perished; and having my car radio change stations by itself so I could hear talk shows that answered specific questions I've had or for spiritual information.

Angels are the special messengers who bring our creator's wake up call to each and every one of us.

Karen's Story

It was January 27, 1995. I had quit my construction job of many years to become a stay-at-home mom, do some crafts, play a little golf, and learn to cook better. I had always worked and I finally had the opportunity to do some things I wanted to do.

I woke up January 28, ready to start my new life. My husband asked me what I was going to do on my first day of leisure. I told him I was going to have lunch with my dad and then do a little shopping. He asked me if I could stop at the hardware store for him. I said sure.

I finished my shopping and drove to the hardware store. In my little town of Seal Beach, California, parking is hard to find, so you take the first one you get. My parking space was in front of a flower shop just a few doors down from the hardware store. This nursery had the most beautiful plants and flowers in it. Every time I walked by the nursery, I always had to take a stroll inside to look at God's wonderful creations. As I walked through this time, I came across three small stores in the back of the building. The store on the right had gone out of business, but the door was open. I peeked my head in, and as I did, I felt like I was being pushed in from behind. When I looked in back of me, there was no one around.

I was puzzled but I entered the store. I looked around and saw a few old pieces of dusty furniture, a lot of dirt, and cobwebs all over. As I was looking around, a male voice said to me, *"Karen, you are to open up an angel store in here."* As the voice was speaking to me, this incredible feeling went all through me from the top of my head to the bottom of my toes. It was like a combination of electricity and wonderful butterflies all at once. I felt like pure love had entered my body.

I said to the voice, "An angel store?" I thought, "I don't want to open an angel store. I want to be a mom and do some fun things." I looked at the cobwebs and dirt and said, "I don't know where to buy angels. How do I start?"

The answer I got was this voice telling me, *"Create it and they will come."* I never saw this angel, but I felt blessed that I was chosen to open up an angel store. On the other hand I felt foolish, like maybe I had imagined the whole thing.

As I left the building, I found a "For Rent" sign behind the door. The guy that worked in the nursery directed me three doors down to an antique store, where I found the woman who owned the building. All the way there, I kept saying, "I don't want to open an angel store. I want to do what I want to do." But I kept walking.

The landlady was busy when I got there, and I almost left, but then the feeling came over me again. I walked up to her and said, "You might think I am crazy, but as of ten minutes ago, I think I'm supposed to open an angel store in the back of the nursery." Her face lit up and she said it would be just wonderful to have an angel store there.

I told her I didn't know where to buy angel gifts. She said (and I will never forget what she told me), "The National Gift Show is this weekend and it only comes twice a year!" My heart dropped again. I could not believe what was happening to me.

I went home thinking my husband would come home from work, I would tell him about my experience, and he would remind me that I had quit a good job to do what I've been waiting to do for a long time. He would bring me back down to earth. Instead, he said to me, "Karen, I think that would be wonderful!"

That weekend, my friend Julie and I went to the gift show just to check it out. When we got there, we found we couldn't get in because I didn't have a business, a place of business, or a business permit. I said to Julie, "That's okay, I really don't want to do this anyway."

We were leaving when Julie saw someone she knew. We walked up to him, and he asked Julie what we were doing there. She told him our story and that we couldn't get into the show. He said, "I run this show. I can get you in."

As I drove home Sunday afternoon, I started screaming in the car. I said to Julie, "Do you realize we got in the show with no business name, no address, no permits, and yet I just ordered over $10,000.00 worth of angel gifts? Some heavenly power sure wants me to open an angel store!" I rented the store behind the nursery that evening.

From the time I had my angel experience to opening the store took only six weeks. Although I didn't know much about retail business, it still turned out beautifully. If I didn't know how to do something, I would just ask the angels. Within twenty-four hours or less, I would somehow have the answer. It was unbelievable. Not once, but every single time.

One day I was wondering how much it would cost to paint the place. I didn't want to go over my budget. Ten minutes later I needed to go to the bank. As I was standing in line, in front of me was a man dressed in painter's clothes. He ended up painting my store. Things like this happened over and over again. I just laughed and said, "Thank you, God."

When I opened the store, I thought that the angels wanted me to be in the retail business for some reason. I saw only the small picture—sell angels, make some money. What happened was that the popularity of the store spread like wild fire. My mailing list grew to 3,000 people in six months!

The incredible thing was that people felt they needed to come to the store. Many people felt a presence around them. We had people who were dying and only had a short time to live have a need to be there. Lots of people came in just to talk to someone. After six months of business, I finally got the big picture. This was a place of healing.

I named the store "The Angel Connection" because I feel the angels are trying to connect with us. I know we are trying to connect with them.

I grew out of my store within my first year. I found a wonderful new place just four doors down the street. It has now been three years. My mailing list is over 18,000 people now. I thank God every day for choosing me to open this angel store. This has turned into my life's work.

There is no end to the different ways the angels teach us. They keep leading us, showing us, reminding us. The teaching may seem very small or stunningly important, but each time it is exactly what we needed to know whether we understood it or not.

After the angels woke us up in 1991, they taught us every day through our writings to them. They answered our every question, explained to us why we had been awakened, and began to give us an idea of what our life work would be about. At first we thought we were quite special because we were getting all this information. The truth is, we were no more special than anyone else, for the angels are teaching people all over the world. It is time to have our questions answered and our doubts or fears allayed from the highest source.

Angels teach. All of the knowledge of the universe is at an angel's disposal. Yet our primary concentration while we are working with you is to help you on your path, through your life lessons, and to support you in your life's work.

We do God's work.
We bring healing directly
from Him.
That is why it is so
impressive.

Chapter 4

God sends His angels to comfort while He heals. Angels bring a special feeling or knowing that everything is going to be okay. This feeling takes away our immediate fear and worry and puts us into a state of hope. This positive feeling also helps us send comforting thoughts to those around us who are also afraid. When the angels comfort us, we are able to comfort others. It goes on and on.

Sometimes the only thing we know to do is to ask for a miracle. Miracles can be hard to ask for; God sends them anyway. Our suggestion is, ask for miracles for yourself just like you would ask for one for your child. Ask for the impossible and then expect nothing. Miracles are miracles. If we knew how they worked they wouldn't be miracles.

We do know this much, however: Angels are the ones who bring them.

ELAINE'S STORY

Four years ago I had a severe stroke. I couldn't speak—all language skills were gone. My husband is a physician and he was scared to death. When he stood beside me in intensive care, the look on his face was so awful, I thought he needed a hospital bed more than I did. My son and my brother were also there. I knew they thought I was going to die because my brother never took off from work.

For me the message came through in my head, loud and clear from my angels, *"Don't worry about it. You are going to be fine. It will take a while, but you will get better. There is more for you to do on earth."* So, I was very calm through the whole ordeal. I could understand what people were saying and I knew where I was, but my mind was very quiet. I had no sense of dying. I was just inside myself and I could hear my angels very well. I was floating. It was like a little vacation inside of me.

I had no way, however, of telling everyone that I was going to be okay. They were fearful; I was not. Finally, when I could smile, and say, "Okay," they knew I was going to be fine.

From Claire in Australia

My sister Joanne was on her honeymoon in Europe when she came down with Meningitis. She was in a hospital in Italy for eight weeks and was unable to speak Italian. We didn't know whether she was going to live or not. When I heard of her illness, I got down on my knees and prayed the hardest I have *ever* prayed in my life. An angel came to my side and told me my sister was going to be fine and please not to worry any more. (I still get goosebumps throughout my body when I think of this.) After the angel left, I had the most beautiful calm come throughout my body. I knew my sister was going to be all right.

The next day I saw my parents struggling with their fear. I told them, and everybody who asked about Joanne, that she would be fine. And she was. And yes, I did say thank you. I always say thank you.

A Letter from Theresa

I have suffered from chronic leg pain for years. After I found out about angels I decided to ask the medical angels to come and help me. I lay down on my bed with my mind blank. After a few minutes I began to feel a warm sensation around my body and I knew that if I had any reaction I was going to lose that wonderful feeling. So I decided not to react to what I was experiencing and just let it happen. Then I tried to open my eyes, but I didn't do it because when I started to open them I had the most wonderful vision of a purple angel flying over me. I felt that if I opened my eyes it would go away and I wanted to experience that as long as I could. I don't know when I fell asleep, but when I woke up, my pain was gone and it has been gone ever since. I have to say that I am very happy with my angels.

SHIRLEY'S STORY

My daughter, Shirl, at the age of nine became ill with scarlet fever. I became very worried and could not sleep. Her fever stayed high in spite of the antibiotics she was taking. She was so weak she could hardly walk. I knew she was getting worse and we might have to take her to the hospital. I watched her closely, asked my angels what to do, and prayed to God. The angels told me to pray and ask Padre Pio to intercede for her and for her healing.

Padre Pio was an Italian priest who had the stigmata (all the wounds of Jesus showed up on his own body) until he died, I believe in the '60s. He had the gifts of the Holy Spirit and his prayers had healed many, but I was not aware of that at the time. After praying, I felt the presence of the angels very close to me and they were assuring me my daughter would be healed. They told me to take the book I had been reading about Padre Pio, with his picture on the front of it, and place it under my daughter's pillow as she slept. I slept well that night believing Shirl would be healed.

The next morning I got up and was in the living room when Shirl came down the hallway to tell me of a beautiful dream she had.

Shirl's Dream

The illness was something I had never experienced before. I don't think I was aware of how sick I was at the time. I don't remember much about the illness, but I do remember a wonderful dream as if it were yesterday. I believe this dream was a gift from God.

The dream began with me as an adult being lifted weightlessly toward a great light. I was not afraid; I was calm, peaceful, and tranquil. Upon reaching the source of the light, I saw that the light came from an incredibly powerful and loving being. Next to this being, whom I knew instantly was God, was Jesus Christ, and Mary his mother. Angels surrounded them. They were at the threshold of a beautiful crystal building (as a child I described it as being made of ice) that reached up into the heavens. Upon entering the building I had a sense that this building was a being within itself, that possessed limitless wisdom and complete love for all that entered. The building opened up into a courtyard of beautiful fields and flowers.

As I stood basking in the beauty and serenity of what I witnessed, a man with bandaged hands, which bled at the palms, approached me. Even though I was a nine-year-old child having the dream, he said to me, "Do you remember me? When you were sick as a child I healed you." I was dreaming about my own future.

I was filled with joy, happiness, and love. This man continued to escort me and guide me through this incredible place. I saw many family members and friends who had died and was relieved to know that they were in such a wonderful place. Many questions I had about the afterlife were answered, and I was assured that all whom I loved and cared about would someday be with me here. I saw many angels, animals, and simple things that had brought me joy on earth. I felt unconditional love and acceptance by all—a feeling that continued after I awoke.

After I "came back," I laid in my bed feeling extraordinarily peaceful, happy, and energetic. My room was filled with a wonderful, comforting aroma, as if my room was filled with fresh flowers and loving angels. This experience has changed my life, and I will never forget it. Since that time I have known that God has sent me a special and loving angel to guide me through my adult life and to keep me close to my Creator.

More from Shirley, the mother

After Shirl shared her beautiful dream and healing, she said she felt better and wanted to play. We prayed together and thanked God for sending His angels and Padre Pio to heal her. Later that day I remembered I had put the book, with Padre Pio's picture on it under Shirl's pillow. I went to get the book to read more from it, and then I put it down on the coffee table. Later, Shirl came into the room. When she saw the book with Padre Pio's picture on the cover, she exclaimed, "Mommy! That's the priest that was in my dream!"

From Christine

A few years ago my life was in a shambles and had been for quite awhile. I was a mess, physically, mentally, and emotionally. I had just left my husband. I had been pregnant with twins and I lost them. I was suffering from agoraphobia, which had plagued me for years. I couldn't do the simplest tasks. Going for groceries, to the bank, driving a car, even leaving the house, were huge problems. I had lost my job and was on welfare. My friends had drifted away, and my family didn't understand my condition, although they did try.

I was at the end of my rope. I felt that God did not care and that He and everyone "up there" hated me. I thought I must have done something horrible in a past life to deserve this life. I hated everyone and everything.

At times, when I did have the courage to get outside, I would go to the cemetery and talk to friends and relatives I had loved and who had died. Finally, I decided I would join them and end it all. I had everything planned out. I was even going to take my dogs lives too, because I didn't want to burden anyone with having to take care of them.

As I sat at my cousin's stone and cried, I prayed one last time for a sign from God that He could show me He loved me and that He cared about me. As I prayed, I saw a Monarch butterfly flying around. I asked God if He would make that butterfly land on me and if He did, I would know that He cared about me and then I wouldn't kill myself. Just as I finished that thought, the butterfly flew toward me and it landed on my shoe!

I knew that my angel was with me. I felt this tremendous presence on my right side and my thought was, "This must be what heaven feels like." It was so peaceful and serene. I remember being able to smell every fragrant scent in the air. I heard every bird singing and I had a peace come over me that I knew was not of this world. My stomach didn't hurt any more, my headache went away, and I was happy. I tried so hard to get an image of my angel but I couldn't. I believe I felt a piece of heaven that day and I am grateful for my experience.

Even though my life is still tremendously difficult, I know my encounter was a real one and it has given me the courage to go on. Most people I have told just said that I was imagining everything. I don't care what they think. I believe I was blessed.

Brice's Story

Losing my career, being disabled, losing my fortune and everything was not hitting a bottom. It only changed my perspective on life.

On September 6, 1993, I was doing my normal morning training run of twenty miles. Eight miles into my run I slipped on a pebble and because of the bio-mechanics of my running, when I fell, I broke my neck and crushed my spine. From that moment forward I was a 5th and 6th cervical vertebrae quadriplegic, which meant I could not move any portion of my body from three inches above my nipple line down. I was completely paralyzed.

I had surgery, and three different neurosurgeons, as well as some other doctors, informed me that I would be in bed for the rest of my life and would require the service of a full-time caregiver. The possibility of even going into a wheelchair was remote.

At this point I was sort of resigned to my condition. All I could move was my forefinger and thumb of my left hand. That was it. I was sent to a rehabilitation hospital where I was finally able to go into a power chair, which I could operate with my thumb and forefinger. I could also use what is known as a sip-and-puff, where you use your breath to control the direction of the wheelchair.

Those in charge of my rehabilitation said I would never walk again, probably never move. But thank goodness I was finally able to be in a wheelchair. I was then sent to the Spinal Cord Institute at the VA Hospital in Long Beach for more rehabilitation. I spent almost a year there and was told the same thing.

After quite a bit of testing, I left that hospital, still in a wheelchair, to live with some friends. I was able to be strapped into a walker that looked something like the Eiffel Tower with all sorts of straps to hold my body in place. That was essential to keep blood circulating. Every quadriplegic has to worry about that.

I went on this way until I was secure enough in my finances to get into a handicapped-accessible apartment. I proceeded to try to make a new life using the Dial-A-Ride transit system, the power in the chair, and whatever other grace God gave me. I went on for several years this way, also going to whatever vocational rehab I could find to help reorganize myself and learn to accept my fate.

I was sitting at a friend's house one day during the first week of December, 1997, thinking about something that had nothing to do with anything, and I heard (and felt) a voice that said to me, *"Get up and walk."* It was a strange voice. I heard it in my ears and I felt it in my head and in my body. It was a tone I had never heard before. It was not an "Arise Lazarus" kind of thing. It was not Charlton Heston. It was a straightforward, youngish sounding voice that simply said, *"Get up and walk."*

Within two hours my left toe began to move. Then I could move my feet. Two weeks later I was up on crutches. A month and a half later I threw the crutches away, and a few months later I began to drive with the help of a caregiver.

I have thought about who that voice belonged to many times. It might have been an angel, but I know it was God. My thought is that He is just not finished with me yet. I don't look at my age group—the mid-fifties—as middle age. I look at it as the second half.

Today I walk like C3PO. But I still walk, and I have a new life. Now I have to figure out what I'm going to do with it.

—··—▪◆▪—··—

Some of these stories about healing may sound like miracles. They may be miracles. We think they are all in a day's work for the angels. Ask your angels for help in the very thing you think is beyond any being's power. Maybe you won't get exactly what you asked for, but you will get what will help you most—an angel's healing love.

Angels comfort when there is no comfort to be found on earth. In the deepest loneliness and fear, we are there, surrounding you with love, peace, stillness, and rest. If there has never been a prayer in your life, the first prayer you will ever make will be, "God, help me!" And He will send us—His angels.

Behind you,

beside you,

above you,

below you,

within and without,

we are with you.

We are there.

Chapter 5

Angels Support

Need an angel? Ask for one. Having a problem? Ask for an angel to help you. Need understanding? Talk to an angel. Need clarity? Ask your angels to take away the fog that blinds you. Working with your angels is easy. Just ask them for what you need help with. Believe they are going to do it. Allow them to do what angels do, and then say thank you for the results.

One day, we had no idea where to go next. It seemed like everything had dried up. We decided to ask our angels what to do and this is what they wrote.

To Do Today

1. *Do Not Fret—God is in charge.*
2. *Enjoy the moment.*
3. *Keep your nest clean and pleasant.*
4. *Do your daily tasks.*
5. *Call your friends.*
6. *Eat well.*
7. *Be with us—as we are with you.*
8. *Notice wonderful things and remember them.*
9. *Be patient.*
10. *Tell someone you love them.*

In the meantime, rest.
We are watching the world and will immediately
report to God anything that is important.

Because we are here on earth to learn, we have many choices. Because God gave us free will, we get to choose how to live our life and sometimes it is hard to know what to do next. The more anxious we become, the more we struggle to find the perfect answer. We may begin to look outside ourselves to find those answers. We want a "mommy angel" to tell us what to do.

Rick told us after a class one evening, "I have always wanted to go to the mailbox and have a letter from God in it saying, *'Dear Rick. I want you to do the following . . .'"* The truth is we do receive that support letter, but the mailbox is inside of us. It is our sense of inner knowing. It is a feeling of rightness, ease, and clarity, which makes the next step obvious.

One time, when we were desperately searching for answers, the angels told us, *"When you get to the fork in the road, sit down. We will bring you all you need to be clear and to move forward when the time is correct."* We believe this today, and we are careful not to do anything until our inner knowing confirms our actions. We, in truth, use our common sense with the help of God's angelic group and their guidance. The angels say to us, *"Follow your common sense—that is why God gave it to you."*

The angels will guide and support you and show you where to go next. If you cannot see your next step, then do nothing. For that means the angels are still preparing the way. Do not ever doubt the angels' guidance or presence. They are there and will never leave you.

God, the angels, and you are partners.

From an Angel Message to Katie

Dearest Child, we love you and you need to STOP!
Stop trying to control everything and everyone! Finals
will be o.k. this year. Make sure that you study and pre-
pare in the ways that you know work best for you.
Listen to other's ideas and feelings about things because
you may learn from them. We're always here. Please
call on us more than you already do. We love you!

Love always, Lucy, Jack and the rest of your angels.

A Message from Cynthia

I was a student in the last months of finishing my
student teaching and completing my certification. In
January of this year it was obvious that the money in
savings and the money coming in just wasn't going
to be enough to support me anymore. I knew I
shouldn't nag my angel, but I did. I asked and asked
for a job that would fit my school schedule and that
would bring me the income I needed. About mid-
month, I received a phone call offering me a part-
time temporary job. This job was perfect because I
could do it on my own time. It was flexible enough
to fit into my existing school and work schedules
and the pay was quite generous. I knew the angels
had brought this wonderful job to me. It helped me
for the short-term.

By March, I was having serious doubts about my long-term employment future as a teacher. One night, I was so stressed out I couldn't sleep and doubts were lurking everywhere. I wanted and needed a teaching contract to begin this fall. I started praying to comfort myself and to unload some of the burden I was carrying. I remember talking to my angel and God until I drifted off to sleep.

In the morning, I was fixing a pot of coffee when the phone rang. The call was from the school district I most wanted to work for offering me a fall contract in the school I wanted to work in most. Angels, thank you, thank you, thank you! I may doubt myself, but after this I've given up doubting the angels.

From Diane

There are angels taking care of my two boys and me. When I was working shifts, I had a really difficult time financially and I used to ask my angels for help. I asked for enough money to pay all my bills with a few thousand left to put in my bank account for emergencies. I wanted to buy a small house for us. I wanted to give my kids a few things that they had had to go without. And then, about a year after I started asking my angels for help . . . I won the lottery! Big!! This is not a joke.

Yes, I paid all my bills. Yes we have a house, and my boys did get a few things. But, I was also able to give $500,000.00 to my family members and friends. I am also giving to two charities that are very dear to my heart—a home for abused women and children and a hospice for terminally ill patients who have no family or friends to help them.

Mind you, even with the winnings there have been down falls. I lost friends and there are some family members who don't talk to me any more, yet I say thank you every day. It is hard for me to believe how much my life has changed. I don't have to work any more. I can be home with my boys. I can spend the rest of my life doing good for people I care about.

I know this is all happening for a reason. I have to stop worrying about what it is because I know I will eventually get the meaning of all this. I really believe there is something else that I need to do and that my angels will let me know what it is. I also understand that if you give, you receive much more. I have asked, I believed, and will let it happen and say thank you! The angels are taking care of me.

FROM GIOVANNA

My husband and I are writing to the angels and keeping a journal. We are selling our house. It was on the market for 3 and a half months and we prayed every day for the angels to bring us a buyer soon. My aunt told me that Angel Samuel is the angel of property matters and we asked him for help. The angels told us that a young family would buy our house around the end of February, and we got an offer on March 2 from a family with young kids.

Then I asked the angels again to guide us to the house we were to buy. We kept driving by a house that we liked. I had a feeling we should look at it, but I was afraid it was out of our price range. It was a ranch house on half an acre and it had a pool. That is what we had asked for.

As of today, that house is ours. I was in tears after our real estate agent called with the good news. I thank God and His heavenly angels for their work.

A Letter from Analee

A while ago I had to take my son to the hospital to have some surgery in his mouth. My sister came along as my support person. It was a Catholic hospital so there was a little chapel there. In Panama, where I am from, when you go to a new church you ask for three wishes. So there I was, praying with my sister, and I asked for wisdom, for our cash situation to get resolved, and for peace. I wanted peace for all our friends and especially for the kids. I prayed that kids will stop killing kids and that people will stop abusing kids. I wanted peace most of all.

We walked out of the chapel and went to the little shop next door to get something for my son. There were Beanie Babies there and I was buying him a couple so he could have them when he woke up. The lady who was waiting on me said, "Do you want to buy Peace?" Well, I was thinking about what I asked for in the chapel . . . that kind of peace. My sister said, "How much?" I didn't connect it. There is a Beanie Baby that is named Peace. It is a little bear with the peace sign on it. They only had one left, and she was kind of saving it for someone special. My son has been carrying that bear ever since.

I said to my sister as we left the store, "Wow! I just prayed for peace. Those angels sure work fast!" Today I realize that peace is there for the asking and that it is easy to have and really doesn't cost a lot. I have never received a quicker answer from my angels than that and it came through my angel's sense of humor. Bingo! There was Peace.

A Fax from Timothy

My "rhyming" angels told me to send you this poem. They said you would enjoy it.

"Angels"

They are from God and carry his grace.
They are rarely seen by the human race.
Appearing out of nowhere making things right.
They offer God's love, wisdom, and light.

I speak of the angels, who come to our aid.
Always are helpful and never get paid.
They're here for a moment and then they are gone,
Leaving people happy and joyful in song.

How do you thank these beings with wings
Who look out for all and do many great things?
It is something I wonder when I'm lying in bed.
Something I ponder, that's stuck in my head.

It is said that the angels are always close by.
When people are down and weary to try
They come to the rescue like a bolt from the blue.
Angels blow away notions you once thought were true.

Angels are surrounded by love, beauty, and goodness.
If you have seen an angel, then you already know this.
Consider yourself lucky to have had such a chance
To talk with an angel and had a long glance.

It is these messengers, these servants and guides
Who show us from where God's beauty resides.
Always have faith and watch with sharp eyes.
You might spot an angel, here in disguise.

From Florence

Even though it feels a bit awkward, I can think of lots of things I want to ask my angels for, but I started out small (baby steps, you know). I know there is a Parking Angel—she gets me prime parking at the mall all the time. I just always thought of it as an odd little joke and good timing.

On my trip to Las Vegas, I asked for a room with a great view of nature (instead of all the limelight). When we checked in, everyone in our party got rooms in a different location. I went to my room, on the sixteenth floor. It was a huge suite! It had a huge sunken tub, sprawling space, living area, and a mountain view as far as my eye could see, opposite the main strip area. I assumed all the rooms were like this, but after checking with my co-workers, I found out they just had regular rooms.

I can't stop smiling when I think about it. It was so easy. What a precious gift of vision I feel like I have received.

From San Francisco

I had been so worried and afraid. I had been out of work for two and a half months because of a bad back. I finally decided to move to another place to save rent. As you know, part of getting a new apartment entails huge deposits. I had no idea how to get money, so I asked my angels for the thousand dollars I needed. Actually, I begged the angels!

One day, a man who lived in my building, whom I knew only casually, came to my door and said he had had a very good day in the stock market. He *gave* me a check for one thousand dollars. He said, "Please let me do this for you. It would make me happy."

This man's name is John. I had only casually mentioned that I was moving but he had no way of knowing how much I needed that check. I wanted to be proud and turn him down, but I couldn't because I knew it would be like spitting in the face of God. My prayers had been answered. I am breathing a huge sigh of relief because I can now move without fear of not having the deposit. How's that for a miracle?

P.S. Later, from another person in our building, I found out that John has helped a lot of people that he felt needed it. He is truly one of life's Good Samaritans.

If you get even the smallest thought that an angel is trying to tell you something, give you an idea, or an invisible hug, believe it is your angel coming to support you. Stay open to the experience you are having. Sometimes we take life so seriously we allow our human mind to negate our encounter. We literally "think it away." You are the boss. Tell your mind, "Hush! I am busy enjoying my angel."

No building ever built, no bridge ever constructed, no plan ever created, has had as much support as you do from one angel. You have many angels. Hundreds of them will be there in any need to stand with you, beside you, above you, and below you. For you are their nucleus.

To Barbara and Trudy from Their Angels

Angels, what do you want us to know today?

That all is well and that you are well protected. Yes, you have much to do and we can help you. Ask.
Ask for the Angels of Organization to come to you and help you today.
Ask for the Angels of Understanding to come to you. They have peace for you.
Ask for the Angels of Wisdom to come to you that you may better understand your work.
Ask for the Angels of Clarity to come to you that you may understand yourself and others.
Ask for the Angels of Patience to come to you that you may follow divine right order.
Ask for the Angels of Kindness to come to you that you may teach and heal lovingly and patiently.

Ask for the Angels of Goodness to come to you that
you will see it in others and exude it from yourself.
Ask for the Angels of Timeliness to come to you that
you may better flow with your own synchronicity.
Ask for the Angels of Beingness to be with you that
you may find joy in your existence.
Ask for the Angels of Knowledge to come to you that
you may understand your work.
Ask for the Angels of Healing to come to you that
your teachings will help others on every level of
body, mind, and spirit.
Ask for the Angels of Discernment to come to you so
that you may see what is truly important.
And, above all, Ask for the Angels of Love to come to
you that you may walk in the heart of God.
This is what you will do today.
We love you, and all is well.

Your Angels, Shining River et al,
and John/Paul and The All

You are part of
God's integral plan
and He has entrusted us
to keep you safe!

Chapter 6

Angels Protect

⇥⇥⟨⟩⇤⇤

Thank God for angels! When you think about it, it is a miracle there aren't many more traffic accidents. When you consider how many millions of people are on the road at any given time, and that our attention is divided or that we are distracted by cell phones, weather conditions, or obstacles in the road, and so forth . . . it's a miracle anyone gets from point A to point B.

The most common Angel stories people tell us are about being protected. The recurring phrases we frequently hear are, "Time seemed to stop . . . , " "I wasn't doing it . . . ," "I felt safe . . . ," "I wasn't afraid . . . ," "This person appeared . . . ," "All of a sudden . . ." After each of these phrases, the storyteller then describes some sort of occurrence that he or she has survived. People feel astonished that they didn't die or get seriously harmed. Many are consciously aware of the miracle that has somehow transpired, and they know that angels played a role in protecting them in some way.

Perhaps each and every one of us has a story about how a potentially tragic event was averted through the help of divine beings. Maybe this is why so many of us believe in angels, because of the common knowledge that they have been there when we needed them. They have protected us in the past, they are with us in the present, and we can depend on them to be there when we need them in the future.

E-MAIL FROM CIF43

The angels have really been working on me without my realizing it. I had just quit a job of eight years. I walked out on my employer without notice, which is not my character. I know the angels will not tell you to quit your job, but I firmly believe they encouraged it because the enviornment was not good and I believe they knew I was headed for disaster. A voice kept saying, *"Get out of there, now!"*

My angel's name is Angela. She told me that she had been encouraging me to leave because the angels will not let you stay where your well-being is in jeopardy, but I was afraid to quit. I was afraid to quit becase of my age, and I am no beauty queen.

One of Angela's favorite sayings to me is, *"Be quiet and listen."* I am one of those people who has to be told over and over again. I do learn eventually. In the meantime, I am glad Angela has a sense of humor. She needs one to teach me.

EVA FERNE'S STORY

On June 15, I went to bed shortly before 10 P.M. I remember rousing and looking at the clock at 1 A.M. The next time I awakened it was 4 A.M. The kitchen light that is always left on was off. The door was open. When I went to call the sheriff, my telephone was dead. Then I tried my Lifeline telephone. I pounded on it. I shook it. It was dead, too.

My closest neighbors are a mile away. It was still dark outside and I am afraid of the dark so I waited until 5:00 to get in the car and go to the neighbors. They got up, called the sheriff, and gave me some coffee.

The sheriff found the telephone line had been cut, the screen cut, and the glass was taken out of my door. The door was pushed until it tore the frame from the wall and the dead bolt gave way.

Where was I? I was sound asleep in my own bed. Surely some higher power, maybe an angel or two or even three, kept me asleep. I stood up in church to say, "Thank you, Lord, for sending your angels to let me sleep." I am 93 years old, and would have been no match for such a situation.

PIDGIE'S STORY

It was a steamy and drizzly afternoon in July. I was heading south on I-95 to a meeting with Dr. Brian Weiss, author of the well-known book, *Many Lives, Many Masters*. I had been waiting a long time for the appointment and I was worried I had not allowed enough time. Was I going to be late for the appointment? I spotted some accumulated water ahead on the inside lane, my lane. Instinctively I slammed on the brakes. That was all it took for my solid and heavy four-door Infinity to lose control. Gripping the wheel, I watched as cars, guard rails, trucks, and lampposts disappeared and reappeared. I expected my car to make a somersault and land upside down in a ditch. All the while it felt like someone was holding me safely by the shoulders.

However, this dizzying voyage ended just off the road, in soft green grass. Even though I was shaking, I was able to proceed to my meeting.

That evening, I reached up to scratch my shoulder. Looking down I recognized a tiny angel pin a friend had given me many months before. I had no recollection of ever having put that pin on my blouse. At that moment, I recall thinking of the miracle that had happened that afternoon and how the angels had kept me safe.

Several months after my miracle, I made the decision to have a permanent angel with me all the time. Her name is Diana, and she is tattooed on my right shoulder.

From the Philippines

I was five months pregnant. It was about 2 in the afternoon and I had driven myself to the mall to buy some furniture for the baby. Just as I got out of the car, I noticed a man coming quickly toward me. Before I could do anything, he poked a long, rusty kitchen knife at my stomach and told me to get inside the car. I had no choice but to do what he said. I began to pray for dear life that nothing would happen to my baby or me.

He wanted money and all I had in my wallet was 800 pesos (about $20.00). He asked me to drive out into the main road. I pleaded with him not to hurt me, bargaining that I would give him whatever I had. As I was driving out into the main street, I suddenly noticed from the corner of my eye a "floating image" descend from above. I then felt a "white light" surround me. It was as if there was this invisible shield protecting me from this man. It is difficult to put into words what overcame me, but the warm, tingling sensation I felt was an assurance that I was going to be saved from harm.

I could hear a voice inside of me telling me what to do. *"Calm him down,"* I heard, and I began to talk to my perpetrator. I calmly told him to take whatever money I had in my wallet. I then pulled over on the curb and dropped him off. I was so stunned I went home and baked cookies! I couldn't comprehend what had just happened.

All I know is that my angels came at a time when I desperately needed help. The parking lot was deserted. No one would have come to my rescue even if I had screamed. My angels gave me the presence of mind to remain calm and alert throughout the 20-minute encounter. I did not share with anyone else my angel experience for fear of being ridiculed, but to this day it is vivid in my memory.

A Fax from James

The angels have been working in my life for as long as I can remember. They have guided me and helped me in many decisions that I have had to make. This story is one of the most recent, and the strongest.

As I was walking to a meeting at my office, I kept getting this internal message to call home, but I ignored it. All of a sudden, I was physically pushed around and it felt as if I was marched to the telephone. I had no choice except to make the call.

When my partner answered the phone, there was not much of a response on the other end of the line. As I talked to him, I became very aware that he was incoherent and then he dropped the phone. It was more than me just waking him up. He was really sick! I tried to call back, but the line was busy since he had dropped the receiver.

I rushed out of the office, telling everyone I was going home. As I left my building, I was amazed

to find a person getting out of a cab right in front. I jumped in, we made every light, and I was home in what seemed like seconds. My partner's fever was 104+ and he was completely unconscious.

I rushed him to the emergency room, where he was admitted later that night. The doctor said he had a potentially fatal infection and it was touch and go for the first forty-eight hours. I was told that if this had gone on for a few hours more, he might have died.

The angels made sure that I called, they got me home in record time, and they were there to help him get well so quickly that the doctors were in awe. One of the doctors commented to him about how quickly he was recovering, and he replied, "It was the angels."

An E-mail from ANGELscrib

My girlfriend and I were driving to Canada. We were returning to the car after a lunch stop when my friend said that she had an inner knowing that her angels had wanted us to slow down a little. The angels did not tell her why, just that we were to delay our start. We waited a few minutes, and then pulled out. My friend laughed and made a comment about how frustrating it was to trust in angels when you don't know their reasoning.

As we drove up the freeway, at seventy-five miles per hour, a brilliant double rainbow, side by side, appeared. I slowed the car down to get a better look/feeling of the magnificent sight before us. We are both in our forties and it was the first time we had ever seen such a rainbow. What amazed us even more was that it was in neon colors.

Five minutes later we saw the accident. We now believe the angels slowed and delayed us just long enough to avoid a flash ice storm. There had been a huge wreck which left eight cars lying in the ditches and on the median strip. The emergency vehicles weren't even there yet.

Never leave home without your angels. Ask them to go on trips with you. You never know how much of a blessing they will be.

GREER'S STORY

I was orphaned as a child. At the age of fifteen I was on my own. I had no education and no one to back me up or help me. It was the worst life you can imagine. But the worst was that I was petrified of the dark. I could not stand to be alone at night, and I had to sleep with the lights on. I kept thinking I would grow out of my phobia, but I didn't. In fact it got worse as I got older.

Later on, after I became successful in business, I had a huge house with the fanciest alarm system that money could buy, but I was still afraid. I hired live-in help so I wouldn't be in the house alone. That didn't work either. I even bought a gun and put it under my bed. I was still terrified. As soon as the sun began to go down, I could feel the terror come up. The darker it got, the more afraid I became. Every night I was paralyzed by fear.

Then I learned to talk with my angels. In one of my first messages, they said to me, *"You don't have to be afraid any more because we are here standing guard over our child that we love."* And I knew they were there. Two great big huge guardian angels. I could feel them beside me, one on each side. My fear evaporated. It was the most amazing thing.

Now, when nighttime comes, I just feel them beside me. I know they are protecting me and my fear never gets a chance to develop. I fired everybody—all the live-in help and the security people. I gave away the gun. Now I live all by myself, and I love it. I guess you could say that I still have roommates. They are my angels.

Susan C's Story

I was alone, driving my car about 65 miles per hour in bumper-to-bumper traffic on the Interstate. I was in the right-hand lane. A utility vehicle, with a huge roll of carpet pad tied to the top, passed me. Just then, the cord holding the pad onto the top of the utility truck snapped and the heavy roll slipped off into my lane. My first inclination was to hit the brakes.

As I remember this incident, it seemed like everything happened in slow motion, yet very fast. I didn't have time to think. I audibly heard a voice shout at me. *"Do not hit the brakes! Take your foot off the accelerator!"*

When the pad hit, my car was knocked up onto the two right wheels and my car became airborne. Then I heard a male voice say, *"Do not swerve! Hold the steering wheel steady!"* Even though my car was in the air, I held that steering wheel straight. When I came down, the car was in the same position as when it took off and I was able to slow down and pull off the road without losing control. When I came to a stop, I sat still for a moment gathering my wits. I knew that if I had done anything but what I was told to do, I would have rolled the vehicle.

There was little damage to my car, actually less than $200.00, which was certainly another miracle. Yes, I believe in angels and miracles.

Bobbie's Story

At 3 in the morning I sat bolt upright in bed. When I looked down at the floor, I saw a layer of smoke about a foot thick. When I got up to investigate, I found that the smoke was throughout the entire upper story of our Victorian house. Looking further, I found a foot-stool smoldering in the upstairs study. (My husband and I have since quit smoking.)

What surprised me most was how "awake" I was when I sat up in bed. It was as if something had pushed me up. Today, I feel strongly that my angels woke me up and saved our family's lives.

Crystal's Story

I was stopped at a traffic light and for some reason was hesitant to enter the intersection after the light turned green. All of a sudden an old Ford truck passed right in front of me going about 60 miles per hour with police cars chasing right behind him. As I saw this, I knew immediately that my angels were with me. For if I had started up when the light had first turned green, that truck would have killed me without a doubt. I was shaken up a bit, but thankful to my angels for keeping me safe.

When I read the newspaper the next morning, I saw a picture of the same truck that could have hit me. It was wrecked. The man driving it had hit a car and killed an elderly man just down the road from where I had been. I was thankful to be alive and, again, gave many thanks to my heavenly helpers. I realized one more time that I was never alone and that I always had protection.

FROM PAM

About nine years ago, I was receiving messages from within myself. They came in a voice and a feeling of someone or something being with me. At first I was frightened, never having had something like that happen before. My "voice" was telling me to go to church because I was going to be in need of God in my life. The message was so strong that I called Father Paul, who was the priest of the church my husband and kids went to. He was a tremendous guide to understanding what was happening to me, and I eventually became a member of that church.

A few months later, I found a lump in my breast. It was cancer. I was twenty-nine years old. I was angry with God! Then a friend said to me, "You don't get it!" Then she explained, "That is why God called you to Him. He knew you were going to need Him in your life." I understood.

MARY ANN'S STORY

My husband had taken our kids to the mall while I stayed home to get some exercise and to get some things done. He dropped our son, Sean, off at a card store while he and our daughter went shopping. They were there a little while when our daughter, who was eight years old, started screaming and crying hysterically and making a scene. This was not like her at all. She is a very even-tempered, well-mannered child. She kept screaming, "Someone needs help! My angels are telling me, Help! Help!" My husband took out his portable phone and called the card store. Sean got on the phone and said he was okay. She kept saying, "The angels are saying, Help! Help! Something is wrong! Call Mommy! Call Mommy!" They tried to call me, but I didn't answer the phone. My family came home immediately.

When they got here, I was unconscious. I had been exercising in one of those anti-gravity chairs and it had malfunctioned and locked in an upside down position. I was calm about it at first, but when I saw myself in the mirror, I saw that my face was getting red and purple. Then I blacked out. When I came to again, I was drenched in sweat. I was so angry there was no one there to help me. I remember thinking, "Where are my angels? They are supposed to help me!" Then I don't remember any more. While I was blacked out, I vomited and aspirated my vomit. When they found me, the doctors said I would have died in a few more minutes. I know now you don't die until it is time for you to die, and your angels make sure that you don't.

———

We have all been helped and protected by our angels many times. It is common to hear someone say, "Somebody watched over me that day!" Or, "The man upstairs must really love me." Think back and remember a time when you were helped against all reason.

In our morning prayers we ask our angels to keep us safe and protect us. Angels will keep you safe anyway, but when you start out the morning with a prayer for protection, you just feel safer throughout the day. They are sort of your own built-in security system. It never hurts to ask for angelic help for everything.

Do not be afraid, but do not be foolish with your life. God wants you to be taken care of so that you can do the great work you were designed to do in your lifetime. You are part of God's integral plan and He has entrusted us to keep you safe until the day you decide to leave your human existence and return to Him.

You are never alone.

We teach you.

We heal you.

We guide and support you.

We protect you.

We walk with you in love.

Chapter 7

Angels Are Always With You

—— ═╬═ ——

Many people think angels are only there for the big events, or when we summon them in prayer. The truth is, our angels stand beside us always. We are their work.

God has sent angels to us to help us because He understands our need for help as we grow and learn.

The angels connect with us in all ways. Watch for their presence and their humor. Become aware of how they communicate with you. Perhaps you have felt a touch or a shiver. Perhaps you have heard them say your name. Maybe you suddenly had a sense of the presence of your angel. Look for their gifts. Become familiar with your angel friends. And never forget, angels are fun.

When you become acquainted with what angels do and how they help you, your life will be better. Believe it.

From Barbie

This past summer I was at a street dance for a local charity. I was standing on the sidewalk, watching the dancers and listening to the music, when I noticed a homeless woman going around asking for money. Everyone was turning her down. I started thinking, with my "human-being" mind, "Should I give her a couple of bucks, or shouldn't I?"

Only a few minutes later, I looked down and there, lying at my feet, were two wadded-up one dollar bills. I casually picked them up and stuck them in my pocket. Then I heard my angels say, loudly, *"Those are not yours!"* I looked around, found the homeless woman, and gave her the money. She never even knew she had been given a gift from her angels.

An E-mail from Kristen

I have been communicating with "the voice" for a few years now, but did not realize it was my angel. What has made the most difference to me since meeting my angels is that now I know I may ask them to help me with anything. I was taught it is selfish to pray for yourself, so I prayed for others. I've always wanted to pray for myself (for things other than patience with my kids). Now I know it is okay to pray for things like making the payroll at work, or coming up with the money to pay taxes. I know I will still continue to pray for others, but I will no longer hesitate to ask for something for myself when I need it.

An E-mail from Pnsy

My main angel's name is Sam. One evening I had an appointment that I could not be late for. The only problem was that my husband was late coming home from work. He kept calling with updates on his arrival time, and each update was closer and closer to the time that I had to leave. Needless to say, I was not pleased.

The last call from my husband said that he would not be home until after the time I needed to leave. This presented quite a problem for me because I have two daughters that I could not bring with me to my appointment. Although I have left my daughters alone before, it had only been during the day, never in the evening. But my husband assured me that he would definitely be home only half an hour after my departure time.

With a heavy feeling, I left the house before my husband arrived home. I was concerned for the safety of my daughters, but I had no choice, I had to leave.

On my way to the appointment, I talked to Sam. "Sam," I asked, "are the girls going to be okay?" His response was, *"Yes."* I asked this question of Sam several times and each time I received the same answer, *"Yes."* But, I am human and trusting angels sometimes isn't easy.

Then I asked Sam for a sign. "Okay, Sam, if the girls are going to be all right, send a car with the letter "A" (for angels) in the license plate. I heard Sam laughing. Car after car passed me, no license plate with the letter "A."

I tried another test. "Okay, Sam, if the girls are going to be all right, send a car with the letter "S" (for Sam) in the license plate. Again, I heard Sam

laughing. Once again, several cars passed, no letter
"S"—no letter "A" either.

Then the highway was pretty much deserted.
There were cars far ahead of me but none coming
up behind. I continued to ask Sam for a sign.

Within seconds, I felt the urge to look in the rear mirror again. And coming up behind me was a car, that surely I didn't remember seeing a few minutes earlier.

As the car approached, I felt my body covered with goosebumps (this is a sign for me that the angels are in contact). As the car came closer, I *knew* this car had a message for me. And as the car whizzed past me, I checked the license plate for the letters. I can't remember what the numbers on the plate were, but the letters will always stick out in my head. They appeared in the exact order I type them here:

"S-A-M".

The license plate was more than enough to convince me of my daughters' safety. But, as an extra bonus, Sam was once again laughing, this time with glee. Those angels of mine . . . what a sense of humor!

FROM GILLIAN

When the police appeared at my door at 11:30 P.M. I wasn't too upset. I already knew I had been accused in a disagreement with two workmen. The police told me that if I came down to the police station and gave my statement, even that late, I wouldn't be arrested in the morning. I got dressed—I had been in bed—and went to the police station thinking I would be home again in about an hour. Instead, I was arrested and thrown in jail. I felt betrayed by the police. They had lied to me!

I am a 54-year-old, professional, single woman who had never had anything happen like this in my life. Sitting in jail was the last thing I ever thought I would be doing. I have never known such fear and humiliation. It was like every bad movie I had ever seen. The place was barren and dirty. I was left to sleep on a urine stained mattress with only one blanket . . . no sheets or pillowcase. It looked bad and smelled worse. I was on medication that made me thirsty and the policewoman guard wouldn't even bring me a drink of water.

Since I was arrested in the middle of the night, it was six hours before I could reach a lawyer or any friends to bail me out. I imagined the worst. I prayed as hard as I have ever prayed. I cried for help from God, and as I despaired, my angel Peter arrived to reassure me that everything would be all right and that he would be with me until my ordeal was over. After Peter comforted me, I was able to be quiet and meditate.

Through the months that followed, while the legal battles dragged on, Peter kept assuring me that the delays were for my benefit and that I should live in total faith and trust. With my angel Peter's help, I have been able to put the shame behind me and the entire suit has been dismissed. Even though I would never want anything like this to happen to anybody, I can, today, see some good that has occurred. I have never believed in my angel as much as I do since this horrible event. I have grown in faith. I also know I am never alone.

FROM JACKIE

I was visiting my sister and was busy doing the breakfast dishes. I had not yet dressed for the day, and was working in my pajamas and slippers. She had taken her daughter to the doctor, and was gone for the morning. As my last cleaning duty, I was efficiently taking the recyclables out to the garage. As the door slammed shut behind me, I immediately knew I was locked out in my nightclothes, in January, in Iowa. It was cold, the neighbors were a long way off, and I didn't know the doctor's name anyway.

Immediately I yelled to the angels, "Help me find the hidden key!" I knew there must be one somewhere, but my sister had a big house with lots of plantings and I personally would never have been able to find it. I needed divine intervention and fast.

As I walked around to the back of the house, I got a clear picture of where the key was hidden. I felt so smart when I bent down, picked up the appropriate rock under the right bush, and found the key in the first place I looked.

SEM7'S E-MAIL

One day I decided to ask the angels about my dog, Jingles, who had mysteriously disappeared from my yard. Jingles was a toy poodle about fifteen years old, and I was heartbroken. She had been with me since I was a child. I asked my angels if they could help me find her. They responded, *"She will come to you by your door while you sleep."*

Following the steps of talking to the angels, I accepted what they had said and made every possible attempt to believe it would happen. Two days later I woke for work and, as part of my morning routine went to get the newspaper at the front door. As I had my coffee, I decided to check the lost and found section and there was an ad for a lost older white female bichon.

Well, my dog was white and old, but not a bichon, but I called when I got home from work anyway. The individual on the phone described the dog to me and I was convinced it was mine. She described everything about my dog down to the type of collar she was wearing. I was excited, but cautious as I had yet to see the dog.

Something was pushing me to hurry and go see her at the dog pound, where she was. As I walked around the side of the building, a small white toy poodle, not a bichon, had her nose in the air as if she smelled me coming. She certainly looked like my dog . . . just a little ragged. As the woman took the little dog from the cage, the poor thing cowered in the corner. But when she brought the dog into the waiting room, she started jumping up on my leg, full of excitement. This dog didn't look quite like mine, but I was unsure and took her home anyway. I soon realized she was not Jingles, but I really liked her anyway.

I adopted the dog. She is wonderful. She did come to me by my door as I slept, just as the angels said she would. I just didn't think it was going to be in the form of a newspaper ad.

From B. Yates

I always prayed to God and believed in angels. But since learning to talk to my angels, I feel a true relationship with God and I don't fear Him. My personal life was so blessed that I often found myself feeling guilty when I would hear of the pain and suffering so many others faced each day. It's as though I thought I, too, should be suffering. The angels have given me the courage to accept my peaceful and blessed status and to be truly thankful for it. For the first time, I don't feel guilty for all my blessings—my incredible husband, my delightful son, and our successful business. It's as though the limitations have lifted and I can rejoice and just BE!

I can't wait to wake up in the morning now—just to see what God and his angels have to say.

Jed's Story

One time I was out on a bike ride and I was thinking about the presence of angels in this world and then I started to have a conversation with what must have been angels riding with me. I was clearly told in that conversation that the angels were always with me and that now that I have connected consciously with them I would forever more have access to their guidance and love. I threw up my arms in delight and felt the wind over my body as I sped down the road. A chill came over my entire body and in that moment I was aware of true joy. To me this is what speaking with the angels is all about.

—

It is fantastic to have a good life. That is what God sends His angels for. To help you have a good life. But good times are balanced by bad times. Angels are sent to help you no matter what stage your life is in. Don't feel guilty if your life is abundant and happy. Rejoice! When your life gets hard, know it will pass and that your angels are leading you back into happiness again with their guidance, love, and support.

Within each of you there is a place of knowing and this place is your connection to us and to God. Listen. Listen. Listen. All the wisdom of the universe is available to you from that place. We are with you to help you. We respect your inner knowing and your freedom of choice. We will not run your life. We do not judge you or scold you, and we will not give you advice you have not asked for.

We angels thank all who share
their story.
Many people think their spiritual
story is unremarkable.
But they are stories of a life.
And that is what makes
them valuable.

Chapter 8

Our Final Message

The greatest pleasure for an author is to receive feedback from readers. That people took the time to share their experiences with us, and then gave permission for us to share those stories with the whole world is overwhelming. Thank you, thank you, thank you! The angels told us before we wrote our first book that each book would touch ten people. Just think of all the good you are doing by sharing your story.

We try our hardest to write books that are non-denominational. The angels are for every religion, every believer, every corner of the earth. If we didn't tell our stories from your belief or point of view . . . then send it to us. We just may not have received a story from your part of the world or within your belief system or lifestyle.

Today, we believe in everything. Everyone has a different background, agenda, and conditioning. Whatever your belief is, we defend your right to believe it. In a nutshell, a spiritual view of the world takes time to investigate. It takes time and trust to look within and accept the inner voice. Everyone is perfect in his or her own timing.

Many of the stories we receive are what others would call "unremarkable," meaning they don't sound very dramatic. Often the event is just a short, momentary episode of angelic awareness that might not sound like much. But to the person experiencing the moment, it is profound. The angels usually don't come to us with high drama. They tiptoe in and our response is a quiet knowing.

We often hear this type of story. "I was driving down the road (or watching TV, or laying in bed, or standing there) when all of a sudden I knew my angel was with me. I could feel her/him behind me and her/his hands on my shoulders, and the wings were wrapped all around me—clear to the front. I knew I was safe and loved and that everything was going to be okay." To read about it seems flat. But, if you have ever had that experience, you know the experience is 100 percent three-dimensional and anything BUT flat.

People often tell us they see angels in clouds. That doesn't sound like much when the story is told, but we have seen some pictures of these "cloud angels." The pictures are magnificent and awe inspiring—truly beyond description. You know immediately that the vision of the angel in the cloud is much more than a coincidental form of light and water vapor. It is an angel. Everyone present sees it and feels the glory of the experience.

We received so many stories that we didn't have space for them all. But keep them coming! We have other books in process and you never know where your story may fit into the plan. The easiest way to contact us is through our Web site: www.ANGELSPEAKE.com. Please, don't forget the "E" on the end of Angelspeake.

Here are some final letters, experiences, and angel messages that we wanted to share with you. Enjoy!

An Unsigned Postcard

I heard your talk at the high school. You were saying that sharing our stories with others would help spread good will. I took courage from the woman who simply asked an angel to help her find her lost car keys. I had many opportunities this week to try asking for help instead of my usual "stinkin' thinkin'." Sometimes the precepts of AA are hard for me to do—but if I ask the angels for help, it works. I shared this with others, and everyone benefited. Thanks!

A Letter from Robin

I was working on getting my friend to go with me to one of your classes, and she said she wasn't interested because it was New Age and that turned her off as a Christian. I told her that there is nothing in the book that is contradictory to scripture, and if anything, I feel the message of your books encourages people to seek the Lord, His presence, and His power even more. I explained to my friend that God ministers to people in different ways and that for some reason, this book's message has made me much more aware of the awesome power of God in our lives.

I encourage you and your sister to keep doing the good work you are doing. The people of this world, with all of its sadness, disappointment, and strife need to know that not only is there a God, but His presence is with us through His angels and I think you teach this very well. God bless you both.

SUE'S E-MAIL

I have been speaking to the angels for several months now. They speak back to me via the automatic dictation, but sometimes actions or solutions would appear by themselves without writing.

After a period of four or five weeks of speaking to my angels, I stopped for one reason or another. My thought process changed to a more negative way. I felt depressed. I felt unmotivated to do things. Three days ago, I sat down and started angelspeaking again. Bingo! I got more motivation and energy to move around and accomplish my goals. I have been speaking to them regularly now, several times a day. I like angel energy!

This book is full of angelic experiences because people learned to ask their angels to be a part of their life. Some people find it difficult to ask. Our friend Amanda sent us this beautiful message that explains perfectly why it is necessary and helpful to ask —from the angels' point of view.

To Amanda—from Her Angels

We are always ready to give you what you ask for. Today think about angels. Think that we are always here for you and all your loved ones. We are so happy that you and your friends are seeking our help. We love to help and be recognized, as that is our mission. We do these things not to be thanked (which feels good to us, by the way), but because we are created by God to do this. This is what we are about. This is our essence. This is our angelic spirit.

This is what you and others need to know. We love to help—that is why we were created in the first place. When we are not helping, we are doing nothing! So, we encourage you and all you know to access us often.

We rejoice at our tasks. Talk to us. Let us know your desires. We want to join you in creating your environment, friendships, and relationships—whatever you want or need. We bring positive and spiritual elements into everything we are involved in.

You get a double angel-whammy in a sense. You get what you ask for (if it is for your betterment) and you get a "spiritual highlight" on top of it.

Amanda: What if we don't get what we ask for?

Angels: *Then you get a "replacement" plus a "spiritual highlight." The asking is key, because no matter if you receive the gift you ask for or not, you still get a gift of spiritual highlighting. Only by asking can we give you the many, many spiritual gifts that are available. They are inexhaustible and forever abundant.*

We want to have you partake of these blessings. The quote "ask and you shall receive" refers directly to this concept. You will always receive something, no matter what. This is one reason we tell you to ask. There is so much to learn, dear one, and so much to enjoy. We leave you with that thought.

About the Authors

Sisters Barbara Mark and Trudy Griswold, co-authors of the widely acclaimed *Angelspeake: How to Talk with Your Angels* and *The Angelspeake Book of Prayer and Healing*, are internationally known teachers, spiritual counselors, and angel experts. Their *Angelspeake* seminars have been featured on many national television and radio programs, including ABC-TV's *Good Morning America*, CBS-TV's *Leeza Show* and *Entertainment Tonight*, and *The Cristina Show* on Univision, the Spanish speaking network. *Speaking With Your Angels*, a seventy-minute video was produced by the Public Broadcasting System and featured an actual *Angelspeake* workshop. Mark lives in San Diego, California, and Griswold lives in Fairfield, Connecticut, where they both maintain their private spiritual counseling practices.